Montague and the Missing Statues

Level 4+
Blue+

BookLife Readers

Helpful Hints for Reading at Home

The graphemes (written letters) and phonemes (units of sound) used throughout this series are aligned with Letters and Sounds. This offers a consistent approach to learning, whether reading at home or in the classroom.

THIS BLUE+ BOOK BAND SERVES AS AN INTRODUCTION TO PHASE 5. EACH BOOK IN THIS BAND USES ALL PHONEMES LEARNED UP TO PHASE 4, WHILE INTRODUCING ONE PHASE 5 PHONEME. HERE IS A LIST OF PHONEMES FOR THIS PHASE, WITH THE NEW PHASE 5 PHONEME. AN EXAMPLE OF THE PRONUNCIATION CAN BE FOUND IN BRACKETS.

Phase 3			
j (jug)	v (van)	w (wet)	x (fox)
y (yellow)	z (zoo)	zz (buzz)	qu (quick)
ch (chip)	sh (shop)	th (thin/then)	ng (ring)
ai (rain)	ee (feet)	igh (night)	oa (boat)
oo (boot/look)	ar (farm)	or (for)	ur (hurt)
ow (cow)	oi (coin)	ear (dear)	air (fair)
ure (sure)	er (corner)		

New Phase 5 Phoneme	ue (statues, continue, argue)

HERE ARE SOME WORDS WHICH YOUR CHILD MAY FIND TRICKY.

Phase 4 Tricky Words			
said	were	have	there
like	little	so	one
do	when	some	out
come	what		

TOP TIPS FOR HELPING YOUR CHILD TO READ:

- Allow children time to break down unfamiliar words into units of sound and then encourage children to string these sounds together to create the word.
- Encourage your child to point out any focus phonics when they are used.
- Read through the book more than once to grow confidence.
- Ask simple questions about the text to assess understanding.
- Encourage children to use illustrations as prompts.

INTRO TO PHASE 5

/ue/

This book introduces the phoneme /ue/ and is a Blue+ Level 4+ book band.

Montague and the Missing Statues

Written by
Madeline Tyler

Illustrated by
Eidvilė Viktorija Buožytė

Montague van Finch is an artist. Montague and his dog Bess have a shop in town.

They have lots of statues and paintings in the shop, but they never seem to sell.

Lots of crowds stop and look at the statues and paintings...

... but they never stop for long. The crowds continue up the street and never come back.

Montague has an art club in his shop.
He helps lots of artists.

They come to him for pens and paint. Montague helps them with carving statues.

Art club is free for the artists. But Montague's rent is still due for his shop.

"We cannot afford this shop," Montague tells Bess. "We need to shut it."

Montague tells the artists in his art club, and they are all sad.

"Montague helps us, so we will help him," one of the artists mutters.

That night when Montague is asleep, he hears some men in his shop.

They crash and bang and argue.
Montague and Bess go to see what
is happening.

"They took my statues and paintings!" wails Montague. "We need to go and rescue them!"

Bess sniffs up and down the shop. She comes across a ticket. The men left it!

"This ticket is for a sports venue.
We must go there to rescue the art!"

Montague and Bess get in the car and speed off to rescue the statues and paintings.

They get to the sports venue, but the men are not there!

"Have you seen my art?" yells Montague to all the sports fans.

"Yes!" they yell back.
"This will help you," a man tells Montague, and hands him a ticket.

Montague and Bess get a flight and
continue looking for the missing art.

They end up at a barbecue, but the men are not there!

"Have you seen my art?" Montague yells to the kids at the barbecue.

The kids jump up and down.
"Yes!" they yell back. "Come with us!"

The kids run up the street and bring Montague and Bess with them.

"My statues! My paintings! It was you all along!" sobs Montague.

"For Montague van Finch, the best artist ever!" yell the artists.

Montague and the Missing Statues

1) What is Montague's dog called?

2) What type of art does Montague make?

3) Where is the first place that Montague and Bess look for the art?

a) A sports venue

b) A museum

c) A barbecue

4) Who really stole Montague's art? Why do you think they did this?

5) How do you think Montague felt at the end of the story?

BookLife PUBLISHING

BookLife Readers

BookLife Publishing Ltd.
King's Lynn, Norfolk, PE30 4LS, UK

ISBN 978-1-80155-071-0

A catalogue record for this book is available from the British Library.

Montague and the Missing Statues
Written by Madeline Tyler
Illustrated by Eidvile Viktorija Buožyte

An Introduction to BookLife Readers...

Our Readers have been specifically created in line with the London Institute of Education's approach to book banding and are phonetically decodable and ordered to support each phase of the Letters and Sounds document.

Each book has been created to provide the best possible reading and learning experience. Our aim is to share our love of books with children, providing both emerging readers and prolific page-turners with beautiful books that are guaranteed to provoke interest and learning, regardless of ability.

BOOK BAND GRADED using the Institute of Education's approach to levelling.

PHONETICALLY DECODABLE supporting each phase of Letters and Sounds.

EXERCISES AND QUESTIONS to offer reinforcement and to ascertain comprehension.

BEAUTIFULLY ILLUSTRATED to inspire and provoke engagement, providing a variety of styles for the reader to enjoy whilst reading through the series.

AUTHOR INSIGHT:
MADELINE TYLER

Native to Norfolk, England, Madeline Tyler's intelligence and professionalism can be felt in the 50-plus books that she has written for BookLife Publishing. A graduate of Queen Mary University of London with a 1st Class degree in Comparative Literature, she also received a University Volunteering Award for helping children to read at a local school.

When she was a child, Madeline enjoyed playing the violin, and she now relaxes through yoga and reading books!

INTRO TO PHASE 5
/ue/

This book introduces the phoneme /ue/ and is a Blue+ Level 4+ book band.